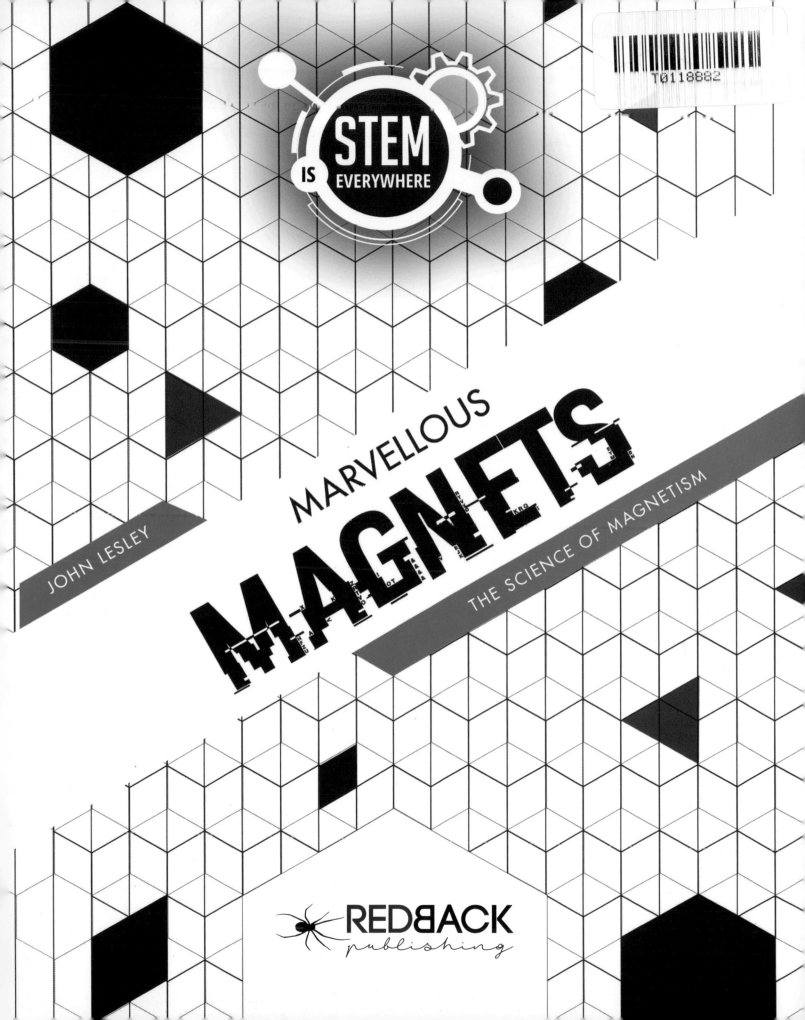

STEM IS EVERYWHERE

MARVELLOUS
MAGNETS

THE SCIENCE OF MAGNETISM

JOHN LESLEY

REDBACK
publishing

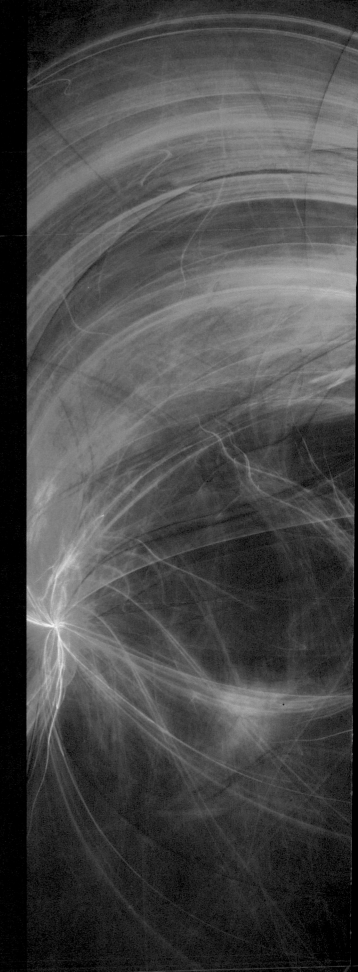

Redback Publishing
PO Box 357 Frenchs Forest NSW 2086
Australia

www.redbackpublishing.com
orders@redbackpublishing.com

ISBN 978-1-922322-85-2

Author: John Lesley
Editor: Marlene Vaughan
Designer: Redback Publishing

Original illustrations © Redback Publishing 2022
Originated by Redback Publishing

Printed and bound in Malaysia

Acknowledgements
Abbreviations: l—left, r—right, b—bottom, t—top, c—centre, m—middle
We would like to thank the following for permission to reproduce
photographs: (Images © shutterstock)

NATIONAL
LIBRARY
OF AUSTRALIA

A catalogue record for this
book is available from the
National Library of Australia

CONTENTS

Magnets **4**

What is Magnetism? **5**

Types of Magnets **6**

Questions and Answers About Magnets **8**

How We Use Magnets **10**

Magnetism and Animals **16**

Magnets and Electricity **18**

Earth's Magnetic Field **20**

Protecting Our Earth **22**

Magnets and the Future **24**

Auroras and Magnetism **26**

Electromagnetic Fields **28**

Safety Near Magnets **30**

Words About Magnetism **31**

Index **32**

MAGNETS

We use magnets every day. From little ones in toys to very large ones in heavy machinery, magnets are an important component in all sorts of technological devices.

WHAT IS MAGNETISM?

Magnetism is a force. It is produced by both naturally occurring magnets and by electromagnets that are created.

The force exerted by magnets comes from the condition of the electrons in the atoms of the material that is magnetic. All magnets, whether they are tiny or huge, have lines of force around them. These lines create a magnetic field.

Magnets have a north and a south pole. Even the Earth has a north and south magnetic pole.

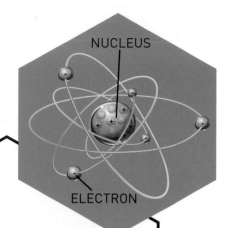

NUCLEUS

ELECTRON

WHAT ARE ELECTRONS?

Electrons are tiny particles of matter. They have a negative charge.

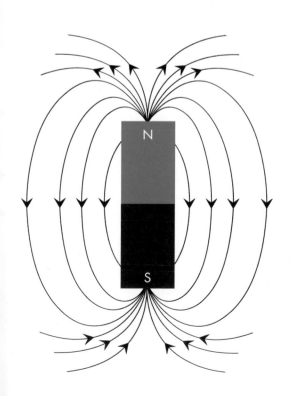

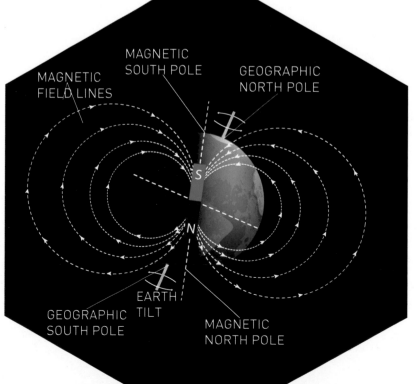

MAGNETIC FIELD LINES

MAGNETIC SOUTH POLE

GEOGRAPHIC NORTH POLE

S

N

GEOGRAPHIC SOUTH POLE

EARTH TILT

MAGNETIC NORTH POLE

TYPES OF MAGNETS

Not all magnets are the same. Some of them occur naturally, while others are manufactured.

MAGNETITE

Also called lodestone, magnetite is a naturally occurring, iron-containing mineral that is magnetic. Large deposits of magnetite exist in Australia and the Americas.

As might be expected, large deposits of magnetite in a landscape can affect compass needles, causing navigators to have to make allowances for the discrepancy in readings when they are trying to find their way.

In Mauritania, the highest mountain is made almost entirely of magnetite. Compasses are of no use on this mountain.

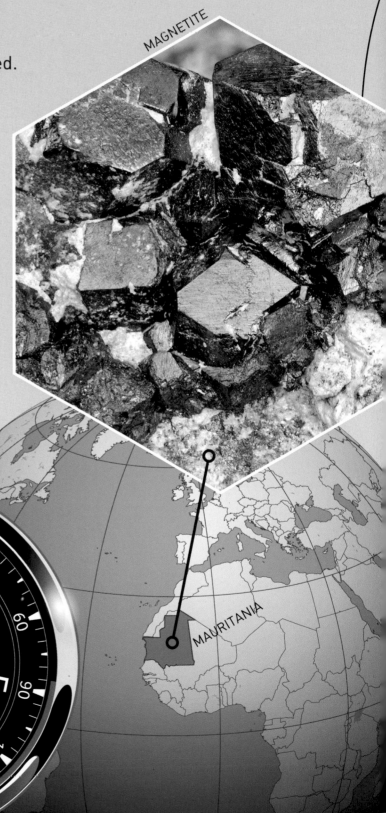

MAGNETITE

MAURITANIA

WIRE COIL

BATTERY

IRON BAR

ELECTROMAGNETS

When an electric current flows in a wire near a piece of iron, the iron will turn into a temporary electromagnet. As soon as the electricity stops flowing in the wire, the magnetism stops.

−

+

MAGNET

MAGNETISED METAL

A temporary magnet can be made by rubbing a piece of steel or iron with a magnet. Try doing this by rubbing a fridge magnet against a steel safety pin. You will find that the pin becomes a magnet too. (HINT: rub the pin in the same direction, not back and forth).

SAFETY PIN

QUESTIONS AND ANSWERS ABOUT MAGNETS

?

Q: How do we know if a material is magnetic?

A: There are a few ways to check if something is magnetic:

1: The north pole of a magnet will attract the south pole of another magnet, but it will repel or push away the other magnet's north pole.

2: A magnet will attract things made of iron or steel.

3: Bring a compass near a magnet and the needle will move.

SOUTH POLE   STRONG MAGNET

NORTH POINT OF NEEDLE IS ATTRACTED
TO THE SOUTH POLE OF THE MAGNET

Q: What if the magnet is a ring? Where are its north and south poles?

A: Factories that make ring magnets for industries can design them so that the poles are in any location that manufacturers need for the technology they are building. The poles could be on the top or bottom of the ring, or they could be on its opposite edges.

Q: If you cut a bar magnet in half, what happens to its north and south poles?

A: Each piece becomes a new magnet with its own north and south poles.

Q: If the north poles of magnets repel each other, why does the north-pointing end of a compass needle point towards Earth's North Pole? Shouldn't it point away from it because it is being repelled?

A: Earth's geographic North Pole is actually close to its magnetic south pole. To avoid confusion, we call both north.

HOW WE USE MAGNETS

MAGNETS AND HEALTH

Many ancient civilisations wondered at the strange properties of magnetic rocks. They did not know exactly how magnets worked, so they assumed they must have magical properties. Since at least the time of the ancient Greeks, magnets have been used for healing procedures that did not have any real scientific or medical basis.

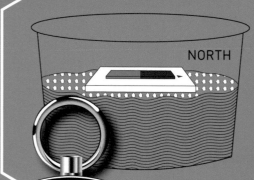

COMPASS

Thousands of years ago, Chinese sailors used a magnet floating in a bowl of water as a compass. Since the magnet always aligned itself pointing north and south, travellers could find their direction, even when the stars and Sun were covered by clouds in the sky.

MAGLEV TRAINS

A maglev train uses magnetic levitation to raise itself off the track. This is achieved by placing magnets beneath the train and on the tracks, with the same poles facing. Since matching poles repel each other, the train starts to hover above the tracks. When there is no friction to hold the train back, very high speeds are achieved.

Maglev trains use electromagnetism. As soon as the supply of electricity is turned off, there is no magnetism and the train stops.

ELECTRICITY

When a magnet is in movement near a wire, the wire starts to carry an electric current. This is how most electric generators work.

ELECTRICITY

TURBINE

MAGNETS

COILED COPPER WIRE

REFRIGERATOR DOORS

A refrigerator door stays tightly closed due to magnets around the edge.

SPEAKERS

The speakers in mobile phones, computers, televisions and earphones all contain little magnets to make them work.

SPIDER

MAGNET

VOICE COIL

WIRES

DUST CAP

CONE

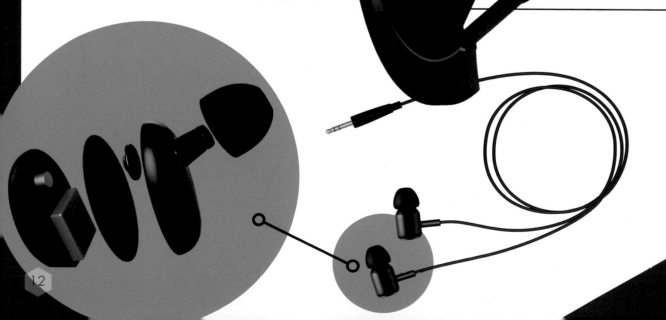

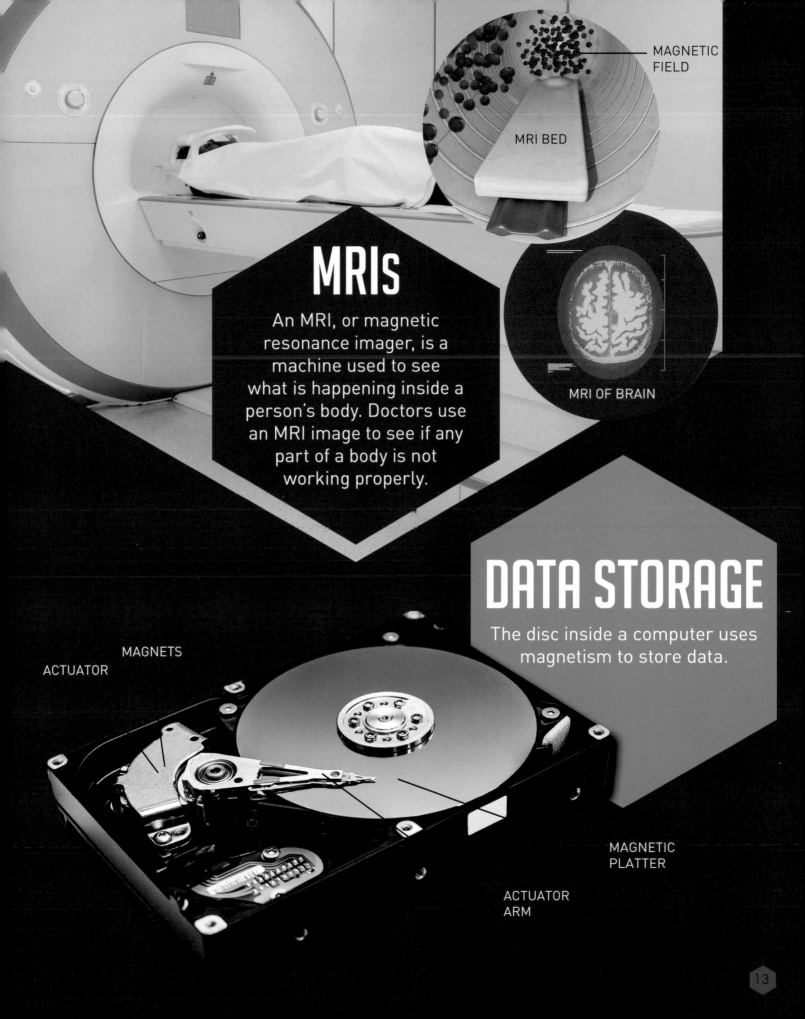

MAGNETIC
FIELD

MRI BED

MRI OF BRAIN

MRIs

An MRI, or magnetic resonance imager, is a machine used to see what is happening inside a person's body. Doctors use an MRI image to see if any part of a body is not working properly.

DATA STORAGE

The disc inside a computer uses magnetism to store data.

MAGNETS

ACTUATOR

MAGNETIC
PLATTER

ACTUATOR
ARM

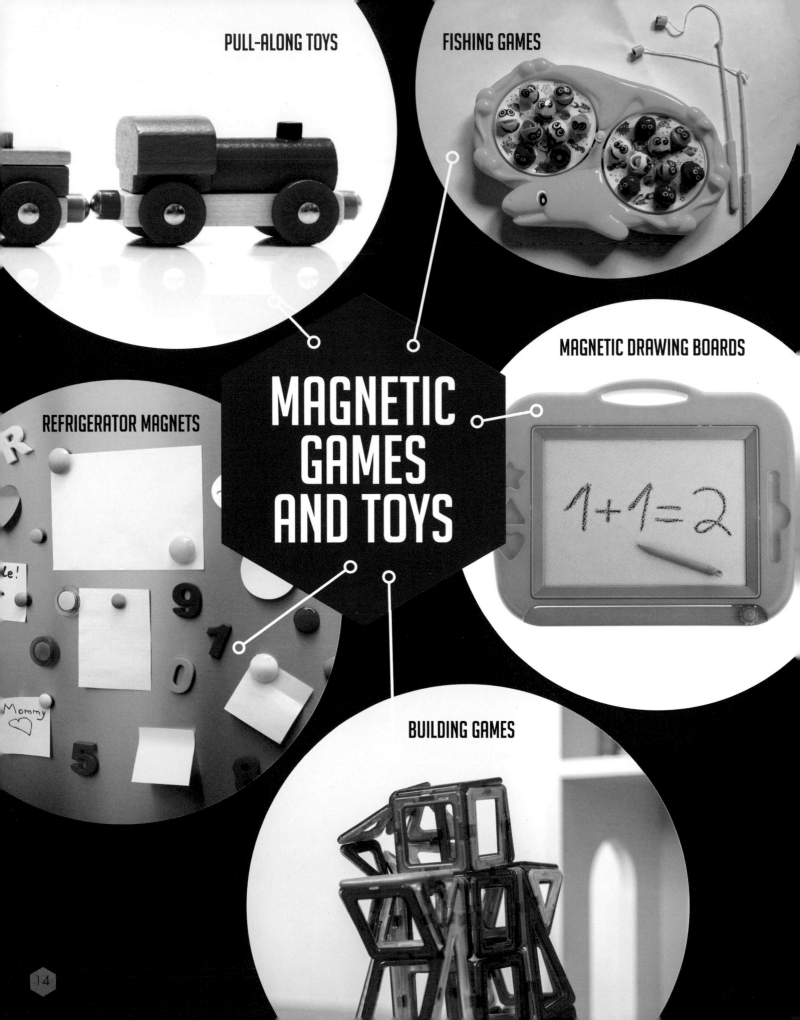

PULL-ALONG TOYS

FISHING GAMES

MAGNETIC DRAWING BOARDS

MAGNETIC GAMES AND TOYS

REFRIGERATOR MAGNETS

BUILDING GAMES

RUBBISH RECYCLING

An electromagnetic crane can pick up metals containing iron from a pile of rubbish. The metal can then be recycled.

NAME TAGS AND BADGES

James

MAGNETS AND FASHION

Designers of clothing and accessories place magnets in wearable items.

NECKLACES, EARRINGS AND BRACELETS

HANDBAGS

BUTTONS

MAGNETISM AND ANIMALS

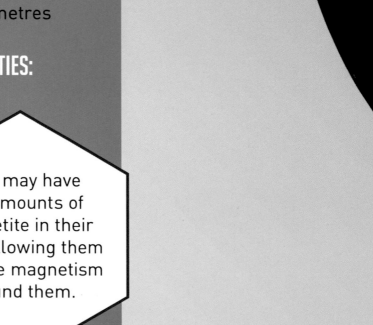

ANIMAL MIGRATION

Some animals travel long distances during migration. Scientists think that the Earth's magnetic field might be helping these animals as they travel from one region to another. Bees, pigeons and sea turtles may all be able to find their way using magnetic fields. Scientists are trying to find out exactly how animals use the Earth's magnetic field to navigate over thousands of kilometres across oceans and continents.

THERE ARE TWO INTRIGUING POSSIBILITIES:

They may be able to see the lines of magnetic force.

They may have tiny amounts of magnetite in their cells, allowing them to sense magnetism around them.

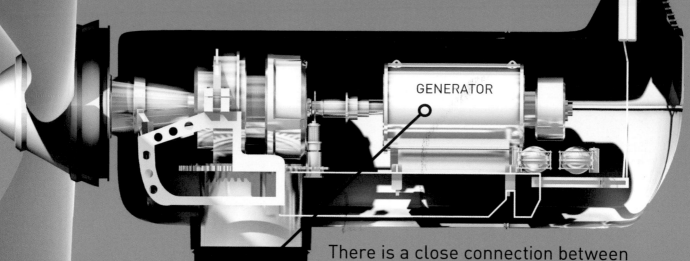

GENERATOR

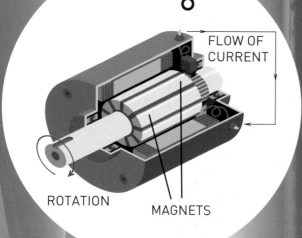

FLOW OF CURRENT

ROTATION

MAGNETS

There is a close connection between magnetism and electricity. Although they are not exactly the same type of force, one can be used to create the other. Magnets can produce electricity, and electricity can produce magnets.

HERE'S HOW IT WORKS!

MAGNETS MAKING ELECTRICITY

If a magnet spins near a wire, an electric current will start to flow in the wire. This is the basis of most of the generation of electricity for homes, industry and business around the world. To make the magnet spin in the first place, a source of energy is needed. Power from the Sun, nuclear fuels, wind, falling water or steam from the burning of coal and gas can be used to make a turbine spin the magnet around.

ELECTRICITY MAKING MAGNETS

When an electric current flows in a wire near a piece of iron, the iron will turn into a temporary magnet. As soon as the electricity stops flowing in the wire, the magnetism stops. This is a special type of magnetism that can be turned on and off. It is called electromagnetism.

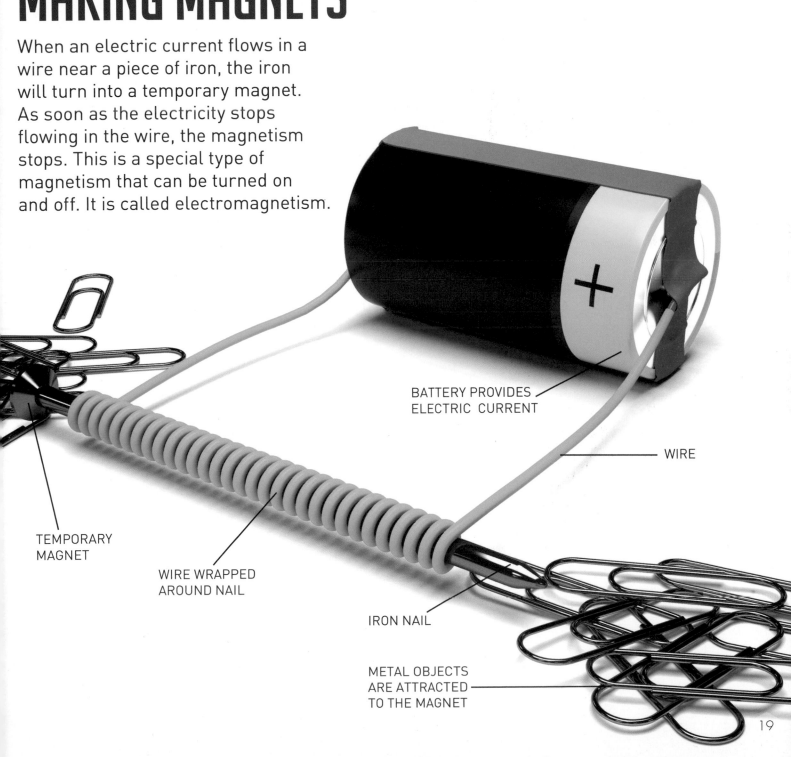

BATTERY PROVIDES ELECTRIC CURRENT

WIRE

TEMPORARY MAGNET

WIRE WRAPPED AROUND NAIL

IRON NAIL

METAL OBJECTS ARE ATTRACTED TO THE MAGNET

EARTH'S MAGNETIC FIELD

The Earth's magnetic field extends for a very long way out into space, and it affects any matter that comes into contact with it.

The interior of our planet contains molten iron. As this hot liquid metal circulates it creates the magnetic field around the Earth.

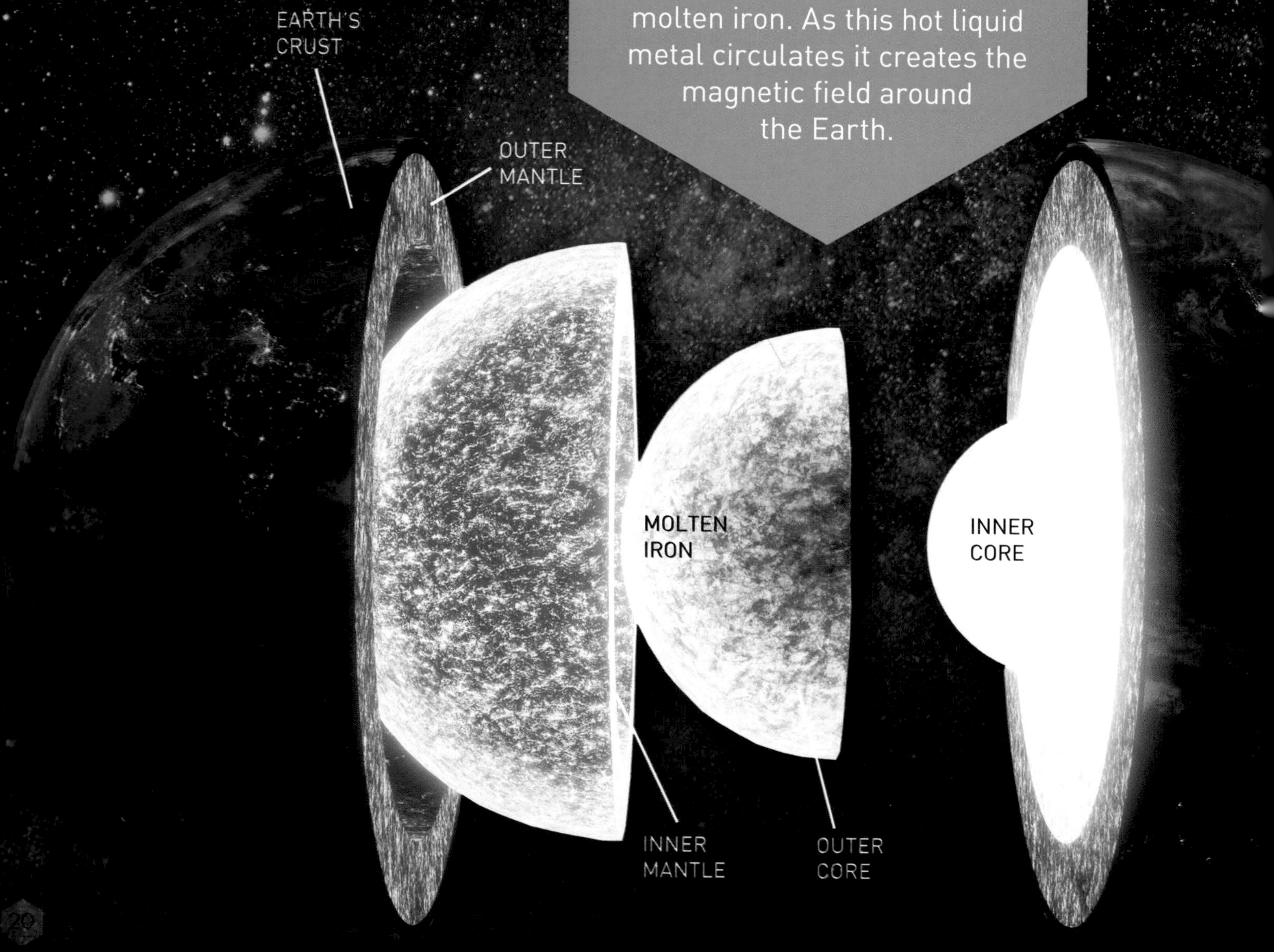

EARTH'S CRUST

OUTER MANTLE

MOLTEN IRON

INNER CORE

INNER MANTLE

OUTER CORE

PLANET

SUN

MAGNETISM IS NOT GRAVITY!

Magnetism is not the same as gravity. Magnets attract or repel each other and some metals, but this is not the force that keeps us all on the surface of the Earth. Gravity causes all matter to pull other matter towards it, and keeps the planets in orbit around the Sun.

MAGNETIC SOUTH POLE

TRUE NORTH

TRUE NORTH AND MAGNETIC NORTH

When a compass needle points north, it is not pointing directly towards the North Pole. This is because the North Pole and the magnetic pole are not in the same place. Presently, the two locations are hundreds of kilometres apart. This makes an ordinary compass useless very near the North and South Poles.

TRUE SOUTH

MAGNETIC NORTH POLE

PROTECTING THE EARTH

Earth's magnetic field has been an important factor in making our planet suitable for life to develop. The magnetic field stops charged particles from the Sun destroying our atmosphere. If this happened, not only would life have no oxygen, it would also be affected by lethal levels of solar radiation.

Earth's magnetic field provides us with a protective shield around the planet. It's like the force field that protects spaceships in science fiction movies.

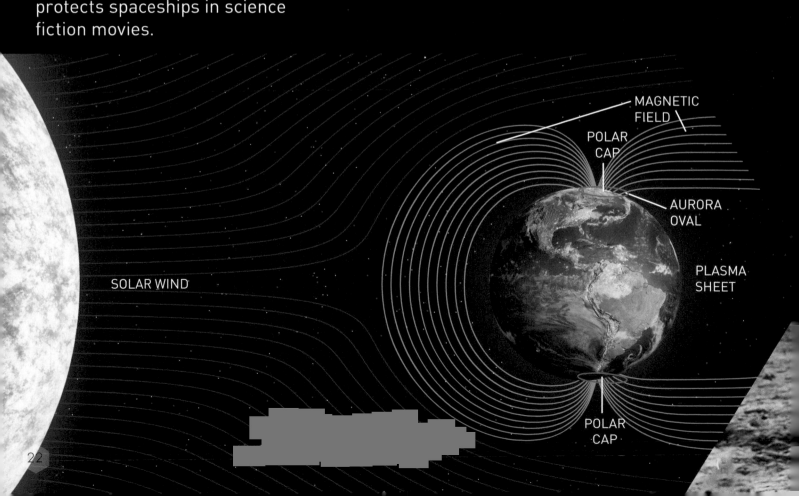

MAGNETIC FIELD

POLAR CAP

AURORA OVAL

PLASMA SHEET

SOLAR WIND

POLAR CAP

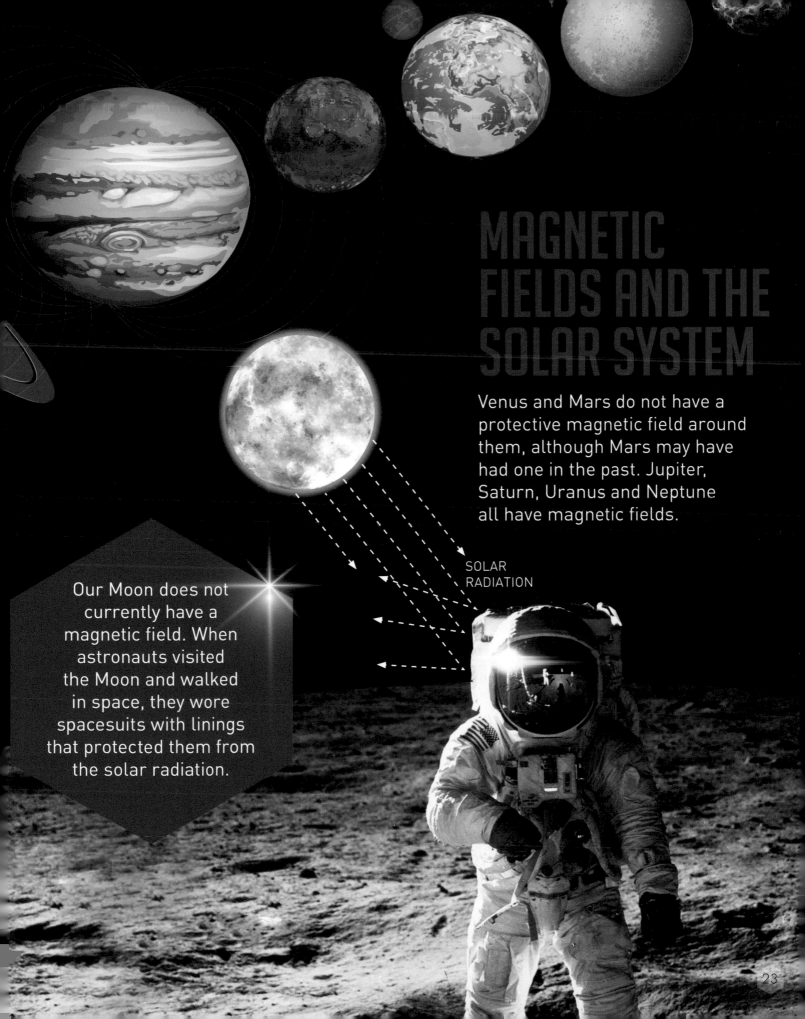

MAGNETIC FIELDS AND THE SOLAR SYSTEM

Venus and Mars do not have a protective magnetic field around them, although Mars may have had one in the past. Jupiter, Saturn, Uranus and Neptune all have magnetic fields.

SOLAR RADIATION

Our Moon does not currently have a magnetic field. When astronauts visited the Moon and walked in space, they wore spacesuits with linings that protected them from the solar radiation.

MAGNETS AND THE FUTURE

Magnets will have an important place in the design of future technology. Electromagnetism and natural magnetism are likely to help us create a range of new technology for fun, work and manufacturing.

SUPERCONDUCTING MAGNETS

A superconducting magnet is a type of electromagnet in which parts of it are cooled to a very low temperature. This results in a strong magnet that can be used in heavy machinery.

LIQUID NITROGEN IS USED TO COOL THE MAGNETS TO EXTREMELY LOW TEMPERATURES

An electromagnet only operates when it is attached to an electric current.

MAGNETIC LEVITATION

Magnetic levitation, or maglev, looks like magic. Using the fact that two similar poles on magnets push each other away, while two different poles attract each other, designers and engineers create things that hover in the air. This hovering is called magnetic levitation. Maglev trains or small ornaments to keep at home can both be made using magnetic levitation.

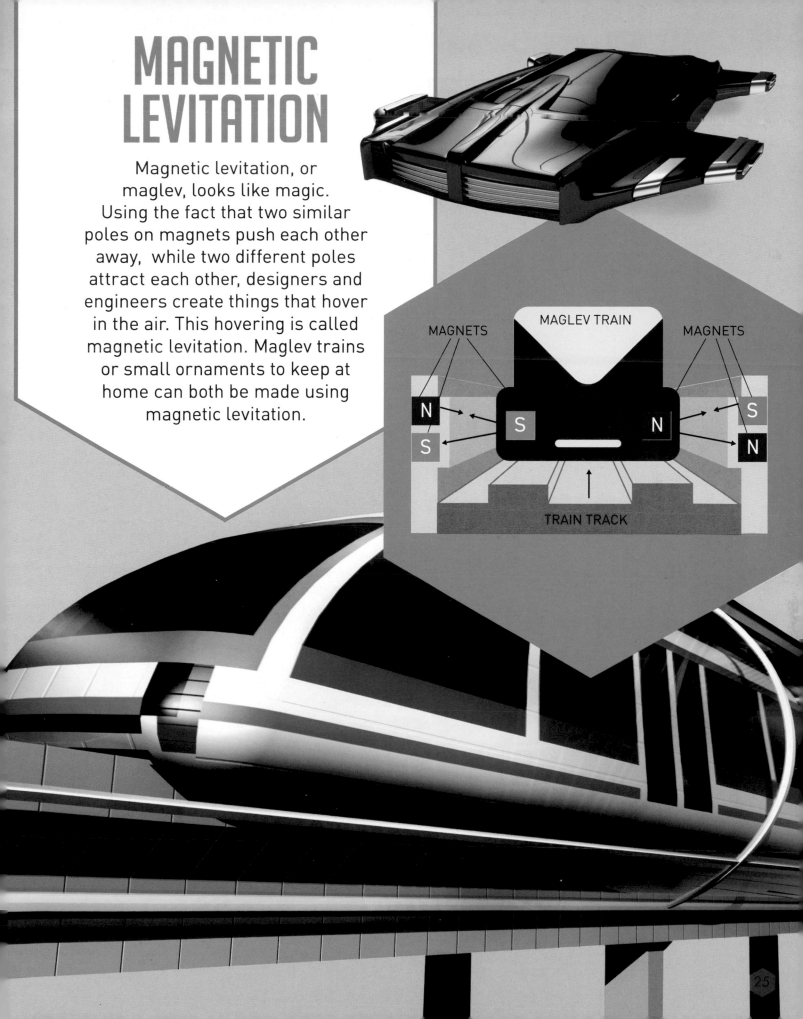

MAGLEV TRAIN

MAGNETS

MAGNETS

N

S

S

N

N

S

TRAIN TRACK

AURORAS AND MAGNETISM

Auroras are magnificent coloured lights that occur in the sky over the polar regions of Earth. They are a result of the interaction of particles from the Sun with our atmosphere and the Earth's magnetic field. The lights of the auroras follow the lines of magnetic force, which is why the colours appear as bands in the sky.

ELECTRONS FROM SPACE

THERMOSPHERE

ELECTRONS COLLIDE WITH OXYGEN AND NITROGEN

AURORA

GASES GIVE OFF LIGHT

MESOSPHERE

MAGNETIC FIELD

EXOSPHERE

THERMOSPHERE

MESOSPHERE

STRATOSPHERE

TROPOSPHERE

SOLAR WIND

MAGNETIC FIELD

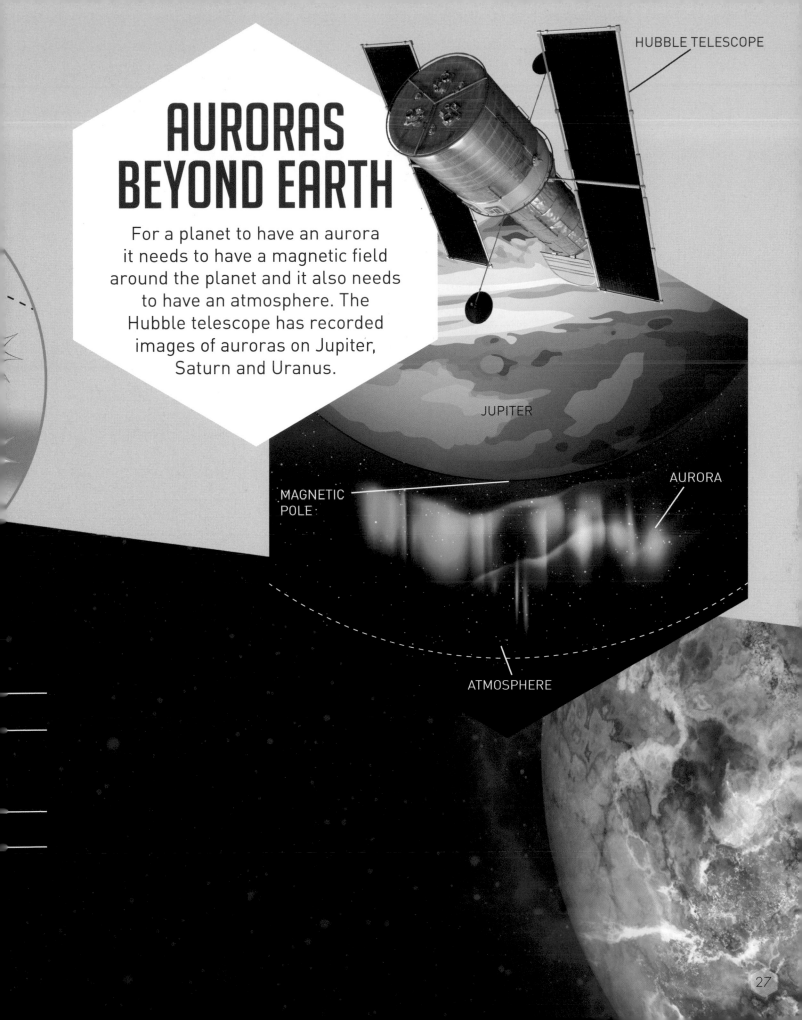

AURORAS BEYOND EARTH

For a planet to have an aurora it needs to have a magnetic field around the planet and it also needs to have an atmosphere. The Hubble telescope has recorded images of auroras on Jupiter, Saturn and Uranus.

HUBBLE TELESCOPE

JUPITER

MAGNETIC POLE

AURORA

ATMOSPHERE

ELECTROMAGNETIC FIELDS

Electromagnetic fields are produced by many of the technological devices we use every day. These types of fields occur when electricity is flowing through a device, and disappear as soon as the electricity supply stops.

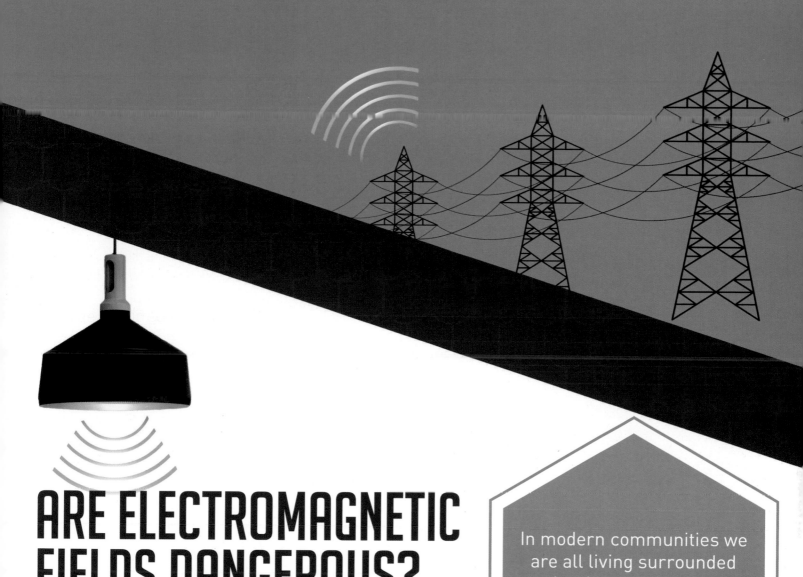

ARE ELECTROMAGNETIC FIELDS DANGEROUS?

Ever since electromagnetic fields were discovered, people have wondered if they were dangerous. The answer to this question is still being debated. The effect on living things of electromagnetic fields near power lines is a topic that many scientists are studying.

In modern communities we are all living surrounded by electromagnetic fields generated by the electronic devices we use.

SAFETY NEAR MAGNETS

PATIENT UNDERGOING AN
MRI (MAGNETIC RESONANCE
IMAGING) BRAIN SCAN

DANGER

	Keep small magnets away from little children who may swallow them.		A very large magnet can crush human flesh that is between the magnet and a piece of steel or another magnet.
	Magnets can damage magnetic strips on credit cards.		A magnet near a compass will pull the compass needle so that it no longer points north and south.

WORDS ABOUT MAGNETISM

aurora   coloured lights that occur in the sky over the polar regions of Earth and some other planets

compass   device that uses a magnet to find north

electromagnet   when an electric current flows in a wire near a piece of iron, the iron will turn into a temporary electromagnet

electromagnetic field   electromagnetic fields occur when electricity is flowing through a device

electromagnetic waves   waves of energy, including radio waves, light and x-rays

lodestone   another name for magnetite

maglev   magnetic levitation

magnetic field   lines of force around a magnet

magnetic poles   parts of a magnet where the lines of force come together

magnetite   iron containing mineral that is magnetic

MRI   Magnetic Resonance Imaging

oxygen   gas in our atmosphere

solar radiation   electromagnetic energy from the Sun

superconductor   substance that will conduct electricity well at very low temperatures

turbine   piece of machinery that turns in an electricity generator

INDEX

auroras 22, 26, 27, 31

clothing 15

compass 6, 8-10, 21, 30, 31

electricity 7, 11, 18, 19, 28

electromagnetic fields 28-31

electromagnets 5, 7, 11, 15, 19, 24, 28, 29, 31

electrons 5, 26

gravity 21

healing 10

lodestone 6, 31

maglev trains 11, 25, 31

magnetic field 5, 13, 16, 20, 22, 23, 26, 27, 31

magnetite 6, 16, 31

Mauritania 6

migration of animals 16

MRI 13, 31

poles 5, 7-9, 11, 18, 21, 25, 27

recycling 15

safety 30

Solar System 23, 27

speakers 12

superconductor 24, 31

toys 4, 14